Income Track

YEAR 1

JANUARY

Date	Source	Description	Amount
		Total :	

FEBRUARY

Date	Source	Description	Amount
		Total :	

MARCH

Date	Source	Description	Amount
		Total :	

APRIL

Date	Source	Description	Amount
		Total :	

MAY

Date	Source	Description	Amount
		Total :	

JUNE

Date	Source	Description	Amount
		Total :	

JULY

Date	Source	Description	Amount
		Total :	

AUGUST

Date	Source	Description	Amount
		Total :	

SEPTEMBER

Date	Source	Description	Amount
		Total :	

OCTOBER

Date	Source	Description	Amount
		Total :	

NOVEMBER

Date	Source	Description	Amount
		Total :	

DECEMBER

Date	Source	Description	Amount
		Total :	

Income Tracker

YEAR 2

JANUARY

Date	Source	Description	Amount
		Total :	

FEBRUARY

Date	Source	Description	Amount
		Total :	

MARCH

Date	Source	Description	Amount
		Total :	

APRIL

Date	Source	Description	Amount
		Total :	

MAY

Date	Source	Description	Amount
		Total :	

JUNE

Date	Source	Description	Amount
		Total :	

JULY

Date	Source	Description	Amount
		Total :	

AUGUST

Date	Source	Description	Amount
		Total :	

SEPTEMBER

Date	Source	Description	Amount
		Total :	

OCTOBER

Date	Source	Description	Amount
		Total :	

NOVEMBER

Date	Source	Description	Amount
		Total :	

DECEMBER

Date	Source	Description	Amount
		Total :	

LIVING EXPENSES

JANUARY

Rent/Mortgage:

Groceries:

Daycare:

Grooming:

Clothing:

Allowance:

Tuition:

Other:

NOTES

TRANSPORTATION EXPENSES

JANUARY

Car Note:

Gas:

Maintenance:

Repairs:

Tolls:

Other:

NOTES

HEALTHCARE EXPENSES

JANUARY

Health Insurance:

Life Insurance:

Dental Insurance:

Vision Insurance:

Copays:

Prescriptions:

Other:

NOTES

UTILITY EXPENSES

JANUARY

Electricity:

Water:

Trash:

Sewage:

Internet:

Cable:

Phone:

Other:

NOTES

DEBTS

JANUARY

Credit Card 1:

Credit Card 2:

Credit Card 3:

Personal Loan 1:

Personal Loan 2:

Student Loans:

NOTES

RECREATION EXPENSES

JANUARY

Dining Out:

Social Events:

Entertainment:

Vacation Savings:

Other:

NOTES

MONTHLY BILL TRACKER

MONTH OF JANUARY

TOTAL INCOME

OTHER INCOME / SAVINGS

BILL	DUE DATE	AMOUNT DUE	AMOUNT PAID	PAYMENT METHOD
TOTAL EXPENSES				

LIVING EXPENSES

FEBRUARY

Rent/Mortgage:

Groceries:

Daycare:

Grooming:

Clothing:

Allowance:

Tuition:

Other:

NOTES

TRANSPORTATION EXPENSES

FEBRUARY

Car Note:

Gas:

Maintenance:

Repairs:

Tolls:

Other:

NOTES

HEALTHCARE EXPENSES

FEBRUARY

Health Insurance:

Life Insurance:

Dental Insurance:

Vision Insurance:

Copays:

Prescriptions:

Other:

NOTES

UTILITY EXPENSES

FEBRUARY

Electricity:

Water:

Trash:

Sewage:

Internet:

Cable:

Phone:

Other:

NOTES

DEBTS

FEBRUARY

Credit Card 1:

Credit Card 2:

Credit Card 3:

Personal Loan 1:

Personal Loan 2:

Student Loans:

NOTES

RECREATION EXPENSES

FEBRUARY

Dining Out:

Social Events:

Entertainment:

Vacation Savings:

Other:

NOTES

MONTHLY BILL TRACKER

MONTH OF FEBRUARY

TOTAL INCOME

OTHER INCOME / SAVINGS

BILL	DUE DATE	AMOUNT DUE	AMOUNT PAID	PAYMENT METHOD
TOTAL EXPENSES				

LIVING EXPENSES

MARCH

Rent/Mortgage:

Groceries:

Daycare:

Grooming:

Clothing:

Allowance:

Tuition:

Other:

NOTES

TRANSPORTATION EXPENSES

MARCH

Car Note:

Gas:

Maintenance:

Repairs:

Tolls:

Other:

NOTES

HEALTHCARE EXPENSES

MARCH

Health Insurance:

Life Insurance:

Dental Insurance:

Vision Insurance:

Copays:

Prescriptions:

Other:

NOTES

UTILITY EXPENSES

MARCH

Electricity:

Water:

Trash:

Sewage:

Internet:

Cable:

Phone:

Other:

NOTES

DEBTS

MARCH

Credit Card 1:

Credit Card 2:

Credit Card 3:

Personal Loan 1:

Personal Loan 2:

Student Loans:

NOTES

RECREATION EXPENSES

MARCH

Dining Out:

Social Events:

Entertainment:

Vacation Savings:

Other:

NOTES

MONTHLY BILL TRACKER

MONTH OF MARCH

TOTAL INCOME

OTHER INCOME / SAVINGS

BILL	DUE DATE	AMOUNT DUE	AMOUNT PAID	PAYMENT METHOD
TOTAL EXPENSES				

LIVING EXPENSES

APRIL

Rent/Mortgage:

Groceries:

Daycare:

Grooming:

Clothing:

Allowance:

Tuition:

Other:

NOTES

TRANSPORTATION EXPENSES

APRIL

Car Note:

Gas:

Maintenance:

Repairs:

Tolls:

Other:

NOTES

HEALTHCARE EXPENSES

APRIL

Health Insurance:

Life Insurance:

Dental Insurance:

Vision Insurance:

Copays:

Prescriptions:

Other:

NOTES

UTILITY EXPENSES

APRIL

Electricity:

Water:

Trash:

Sewage:

Internet:

Cable:

Phone:

Other:

NOTES

DEBTS

APRIL

Credit Card 1:

Credit Card 2:

Credit Card 3:

Personal Loan 1:

Personal Loan 2:

Student Loans:

NOTES

RECREATION EXPENSES

APRIL

Dining Out:

Social Events:

Entertainment:

Vacation Savings:

Other:

NOTES

MONTHLY BILL TRACKER

MONTH OF APRIL

TOTAL INCOME

OTHER INCOME / SAVINGS

BILL	DUE DATE	AMOUNT DUE	AMOUNT PAID	PAYMENT METHOD
TOTAL EXPENSES				

LIVING EXPENSES

MAY

Rent/Mortgage:

Groceries:

Daycare:

Grooming:

Clothing:

Allowance:

Tuition:

Other:

NOTES

TRANSPORTATION EXPENSES

MAY

Car Note:

Gas:

Maintenance:

Repairs:

Tolls:

Other:

NOTES

HEALTHCARE EXPENSES

MAY

Health Insurance:

Life Insurance:

Dental Insurance:

Vision Insurance:

Copays:

Prescriptions:

Other:

NOTES

UTILITY EXPENSES

MAY

Electricity:

Water:

Trash:

Sewage:

Internet:

Cable:

Phone:

Other:

NOTES

DEBTS

MAY

Credit Card 1:

Credit Card 2:

Credit Card 3:

Personal Loan 1:

Personal Loan 2:

Student Loans:

NOTES

RECREATION EXPENSES

MAY

Dining Out:

Social Events:

Entertainment:

Vacation Savings:

Other:

NOTES

MONTHLY BILL TRACKER

MONTH OF MAY				
TOTAL INCOME		**OTHER INCOME / SAVINGS**		
BILL	**DUE DATE**	**AMOUNT DUE**	**AMOUNT PAID**	**PAYMENT METHOD**
TOTAL EXPENSES				

LIVING EXPENSES

JUNE

Rent/Mortgage:

Groceries:

Daycare:

Grooming:

Clothing:

Allowance:

Tuition:

Other:

NOTES

TRANSPORTATION EXPENSES

JUNE

Car Note:

Gas:

Maintenance:

Repairs:

Tolls:

Other:

NOTES

HEALTHCARE EXPENSES

JUNE

Health Insurance:

Life Insurance:

Dental Insurance:

Vision Insurance:

Copays:

Prescriptions:

Other:

NOTES

UTILITY EXPENSES

JUNE

Electricity:

Water:

Trash:

Sewage:

Internet:

Cable:

Phone:

Other:

NOTES

DEBTS

JUNE

Credit Card 1:

Credit Card 2:

Credit Card 3:

Personal Loan 1:

Personal Loan 2:

Student Loans:

NOTES

RECREATION EXPENSES

JUNE

Dining Out:

Social Events:

Entertainment:

Vacation Savings:

Other:

NOTES

MONTHLY BILL TRACKER

MONTH OF JUNE				

TOTAL INCOME		OTHER INCOME / SAVINGS		

BILL	DUE DATE	AMOUNT DUE	AMOUNT PAID	PAYMENT METHOD
TOTAL EXPENSES				

LIVING EXPENSES

JULY

Rent/Mortgage:

Groceries:

Daycare:

Grooming:

Clothing:

Allowance:

Tuition:

Other:

NOTES

TRANSPORTATION EXPENSES

JULY

Car Note:

Gas:

Maintenance:

Repairs:

Tolls:

Other:

NOTES

HEALTHCARE EXPENSES

JULY

Health Insurance: ....

Life Insurance: ....

Dental Insurance: ....

Vision Insurance: ....

Copays: ....

Prescriptions: ....

Other: ....

....

....

....

....

NOTES

UTILITY EXPENSES

JULY

Electricity: _____

Water: _____

Trash: _____

Sewage: _____

Internet: _____

Cable: _____

Phone: _____

Other: ....

....

....

....

NOTES

DEBTS

JULY

Credit Card 1:

Credit Card 2:

Credit Card 3:

Personal Loan 1:

Personal Loan 2:

Student Loans:

NOTES

RECREATION EXPENSES

JULY

Dining Out:

Social Events:

Entertainment:

Vacation Savings:

Other:

NOTES

MONTHLY BILL TRACKER

MONTH OF JULY

TOTAL INCOME

OTHER INCOME / SAVINGS

BILL	DUE DATE	AMOUNT DUE	AMOUNT PAID	PAYMENT METHOD
TOTAL EXPENSES				

LIVING EXPENSES

AUGUST

Rent/Mortgage:

Groceries:

Daycare:

Grooming:

Clothing:

Allowance:

Tuition:

Other:

NOTES

TRANSPORTATION EXPENSES

AUGUST

Car Note:

Gas:

Maintenance:

Repairs:

Tolls:

Other:

NOTES

HEALTHCARE EXPENSES

AUGUST

Health Insurance:

Life Insurance:

Dental Insurance:

Vision Insurance:

Copays:

Prescriptions:

Other:

NOTES

UTILITY EXPENSES

AUGUST

Electricity:

Water:

Trash:

Sewage:

Internet:

Cable:

Phone:

Other:

NOTES

DEBTS

AUGUST

Credit Card 1:

Credit Card 2:

Credit Card 3:

Personal Loan 1:

Personal Loan 2:

Student Loans:

NOTES

RECREATION EXPENSES

AUGUST

Dining Out:

Social Events:

Entertainment:

Vacation Savings:

Other:

NOTES

MONTHLY BILL TRACKER

MONTH OF AUGUST

TOTAL INCOME		OTHER INCOME / SAVINGS		

BILL	DUE DATE	AMOUNT DUE	AMOUNT PAID	PAYMENT METHOD
TOTAL EXPENSES				

LIVING EXPENSES

SEPTEMBER

Rent/Mortgage:

Groceries:

Daycare:

Grooming:

Clothing:

Allowance:

Tuition:

Other:

NOTES

TRANSPORTATION EXPENSES

SEPTEMBER

Car Note:

Gas:

Maintenance:

Repairs:

Tolls:

Other:

NOTES

HEALTHCARE EXPENSES

SEPTEMBER

Health Insurance:

Life Insurance:

Dental Insurance:

Vision Insurance:

Copays:

Prescriptions:

Other:

NOTES

UTILITY EXPENSES

SEPTEMBER

Electricity:

Water:

Trash:

Sewage:

Internet:

Cable:

Phone:

Other:

NOTES

DEBTS

SEPTEMBER

Credit Card 1:

Credit Card 2:

Credit Card 3:

Personal Loan 1:

Personal Loan 2:

Student Loans:

NOTES

RECREATION EXPENSES

SEPTEMBER

Dining Out:

Social Events:

Entertainment:

Vacation Savings:

Other:

NOTES

MONTHLY BILL TRACKER

TOTAL INCOME		OTHER INCOME / SAVINGS		
BILL	**DUE DATE**	**AMOUNT DUE**	**AMOUNT PAID**	**PAYMENT METHOD**
TOTAL EXPENSES				

LIVING EXPENSES

OCTOBER

Rent/Mortgage:

Groceries:

Daycare:

Grooming:

Clothing:

Allowance:

Tuition:

Other:

NOTES

TRANSPORTATION EXPENSES

OCTOBER

Car Note:

Gas:

Maintenance:

Repairs:

Tolls:

Other:

NOTES

HEALTHCARE EXPENSES

OCTOBER

Health Insurance:

Life Insurance:

Dental Insurance:

Vision Insurance:

Copays:

Prescriptions:

Other:

NOTES

UTILITY EXPENSES

OCTOBER

Electricity:

Water:

Trash:

Sewage:

Internet:

Cable:

Phone:

Other:

NOTES

DEBTS

OCTOBER

Credit Card 1:

Credit Card 2:

Credit Card 3:

Personal Loan 1:

Personal Loan 2:

Student Loans:

NOTES

RECREATION EXPENSES

OCTOBER

Dining Out:

Social Events:

Entertainment:

Vacation Savings:

Other:

NOTES

MONTHLY BILL TRACKER

MONTH OF OCTOBER

TOTAL INCOME

OTHER INCOME / SAVINGS

BILL	DUE DATE	AMOUNT DUE	AMOUNT PAID	PAYMENT METHOD
TOTAL EXPENSES				

LIVING EXPENSES

NOVEMBER

Rent/Mortgage:

Groceries:

Daycare:

Grooming:

Clothing:

Allowance:

Tuition:

Other:

NOTES

TRANSPORTATION EXPENSES

NOVEMBER

Car Note:

Gas:

Maintenance:

Repairs:

Tolls:

Other:

NOTES

HEALTHCARE EXPENSES

NOVEMBER

Health Insurance:

Life Insurance:

Dental Insurance:

Vision Insurance:

Copays:

Prescriptions:

Other:

NOTES

UTILITY EXPENSES

NOVEMBER

Electricity:

Water:

Trash:

Sewage:

Internet:

Cable:

Phone:

Other:

NOTES

DEBTS

NOVEMBER

Credit Card 1:

Credit Card 2:

Credit Card 3:

Personal Loan 1:

Personal Loan 2:

Student Loans:

NOTES

RECREATION EXPENSES

NOVEMBER

Dining Out:

Social Events:

Entertainment:

Vacation Savings:

Other:

NOTES

MONTHLY BILL TRACKER

MONTH OF NOVEMBER				
TOTAL INCOME		**OTHER INCOME / SAVINGS**		
BILL	DUE DATE	AMOUNT DUE	AMOUNT PAID	PAYMENT METHOD
TOTAL EXPENSES				

LIVING EXPENSES

DECEMBER

Rent/Mortgage:

Groceries:

Daycare:

Grooming:

Clothing:

Allowance:

Tuition:

Other:

NOTES

TRANSPORTATION EXPENSES

DECEMBER

Car Note:

Gas:

Maintenance:

Repairs:

Tolls:

Other:

NOTES

HEALTHCARE EXPENSES

DECEMBER

Health Insurance:

Life Insurance:

Dental Insurance:

Vision Insurance:

Copays:

Prescriptions:

Other:

NOTES

UTILITY EXPENSES

DECEMBER

Electricity:

Water:

Trash:

Sewage:

Internet:

Cable:

Phone:

Other:

NOTES

DEBTS

DECEMBER

Credit Card 1:

Credit Card 2:

Credit Card 3:

Personal Loan 1:

Personal Loan 2:

Student Loans:

NOTES

RECREATION EXPENSES

DECEMBER

Dining Out:

Social Events:

Entertainment:

Vacation Savings:

Other:

NOTES

MONTHLY BILL TRACKER

MONTH OF DECEMBER

TOTAL INCOME			OTHER INCOME / SAVINGS	

BILL	DUE DATE	AMOUNT DUE	AMOUNT PAID	PAYMENT METHOD
TOTAL EXPENSES				

LIVING EXPENSES

JANUARY

Rent/Mortgage:

Groceries:

Daycare:

Grooming:

Clothing:

Allowance:

Tuition:

Other:

NOTES

TRANSPORTATION EXPENSES

JANUARY

Car Note:

Gas:

Maintenance:

Repairs:

Tolls:

Other:

NOTES

HEALTHCARE EXPENSES

JANUARY

Health Insurance:

Life Insurance:

Dental Insurance:

Vision Insurance:

Copays:

Prescriptions:

Other:

NOTES

UTILITY EXPENSES

JANUARY

Electricity:

Water:

Trash:

Sewage:

Internet:

Cable:

Phone:

Other:

NOTES

DEBTS

JANUARY

Credit Card 1:

Credit Card 2:

Credit Card 3:

Personal Loan 1:

Personal Loan 2:

Student Loans:

NOTES

RECREATION EXPENSES

JANUARY

Dining Out:

Social Events:

Entertainment:

Vacation Savings:

Other:

NOTES

MONTHLY BILL TRACKER

MONTH OF JANUARY

TOTAL INCOME

OTHER INCOME / SAVINGS

BILL	DUE DATE	AMOUNT DUE	AMOUNT PAID	PAYMENT METHOD
TOTAL EXPENSES				

LIVING EXPENSES

FEBRUARY

Rent/Mortgage:

Groceries:

Daycare:

Grooming:

Clothing:

Allowance:

Tuition:

Other:

NOTES

TRANSPORTATION EXPENSES

FEBRUARY

Car Note:

Gas:

Maintenance:

Repairs:

Tolls:

Other:

NOTES

HEALTHCARE EXPENSES

FEBRUARY

Health Insurance:

Life Insurance:

Dental Insurance:

Vision Insurance:

Copays:

Prescriptions:

Other:

NOTES

UTILITY EXPENSES

FEBRUARY

Electricity:

Water:

Trash:

Sewage:

Internet:

Cable:

Phone:

Other:

NOTES

DEBTS

FEBRUARY

Credit Card 1:

Credit Card 2:

Credit Card 3:

Personal Loan 1:

Personal Loan 2:

Student Loans:

NOTES

RECREATION EXPENSES

FEBRUARY

Dining Out:

Social Events:

Entertainment:

Vacation Savings:

Other:

NOTES

MONTHLY BILL TRACKER

MONTH OF FEBRUARY

TOTAL INCOME

OTHER INCOME / SAVINGS

BILL	DUE DATE	AMOUNT DUE	AMOUNT PAID	PAYMENT METHOD
TOTAL EXPENSES				

LIVING EXPENSES

MARCH

Rent/Mortgage:

Groceries:

Daycare:

Grooming:

Clothing:

Allowance:

Tuition:

Other:

NOTES

TRANSPORTATION EXPENSES

MARCH

Car Note:

Gas:

Maintenance:

Repairs:

Tolls:

Other:

NOTES

HEALTHCARE EXPENSES

MARCH

Health Insurance: ....

Life Insurance: ....

Dental Insurance: ....

Vision Insurance: ....

Copays: ....

Prescriptions: ....

Other: ....

....

....

....

NOTES

UTILITY EXPENSES

MARCH

....

Electricity: ....

Water: ....

Trash: ....

Sewage: ....

Internet: ....

Cable: ....

Phone: ....

Other: ....

....

....

....

NOTES

DEBTS

MARCH

Credit Card 1:

Credit Card 2:

Credit Card 3:

Personal Loan 1:

Personal Loan 2:

Student Loans:

NOTES

RECREATION EXPENSES

MARCH

Dining Out:

Social Events:

Entertainment:

Vacation Savings:

Other:

NOTES

MONTHLY BILL TRACKER

MONTH OF MARCH				
TOTAL INCOME		OTHER INCOME / SAVINGS		

BILL	DUE DATE	AMOUNT DUE	AMOUNT PAID	PAYMENT METHOD
TOTAL EXPENSES				

LIVING EXPENSES

APRIL

Rent/Mortgage:

Groceries:

Daycare:

Grooming:

Clothing:

Allowance:

Tuition:

Other:

NOTES

TRANSPORTATION EXPENSES

APRIL

Car Note:

Gas:

Maintenance:

Repairs:

Tolls:

Other:

NOTES

HEALTHCARE EXPENSES

APRIL

Health Insurance:

Life Insurance:

Dental Insurance:

Vision Insurance:

Copays:

Prescriptions:

Other:

NOTES

UTILITY EXPENSES

APRIL

Electricity:

Water:

Trash:

Sewage:

Internet:

Cable:

Phone:

Other:

NOTES

DEBTS

APRIL

Credit Card 1:

Credit Card 2:

Credit Card 3:

Personal Loan 1:

Personal Loan 2:

Student Loans:

NOTES

RECREATION EXPENSES

APRIL

Dining Out:

Social Events:

Entertainment:

Vacation Savings:

Other:

NOTES

MONTHLY BILL TRACKER

MONTH OF APRIL

TOTAL INCOME

OTHER INCOME / SAVINGS

BILL	DUE DATE	AMOUNT DUE	AMOUNT PAID	PAYMENT METHOD
TOTAL EXPENSES				

LIVING EXPENSES

MAY

Rent/Mortgage:

Groceries:

Daycare:

Grooming:

Clothing:

Allowance:

Tuition:

Other:

NOTES

TRANSPORTATION EXPENSES

MAY

Car Note:

Gas:

Maintenance:

Repairs:

Tolls:

Other:

NOTES

HEALTHCARE EXPENSES

MAY

Health Insurance: ....

Life Insurance: ....

Dental Insurance: ....

Vision Insurance: ....

Copays: ....

Prescriptions: ....

Other: ....

....

....

....

....

NOTES

UTILITY EXPENSES

MAY

Electricity: ....

Water: ....

Trash: ....

Sewage: ....

Internet: ....

Cable: ....

Phone: ....

Other: ....

....

....

....

NOTES

DEBTS

MAY

Credit Card 1:

Credit Card 2:

Credit Card 3:

Personal Loan 1:

Personal Loan 2:

Student Loans:

NOTES

RECREATION EXPENSES

MAY

Dining Out:

Social Events:

Entertainment:

Vacation Savings:

Other:

NOTES

MONTHLY BILL TRACKER

MONTH OF MAY

TOTAL INCOME   **OTHER INCOME / SAVINGS**

BILL	DUE DATE	AMOUNT DUE	AMOUNT PAID	PAYMENT METHOD
TOTAL EXPENSES				

LIVING EXPENSES

JUNE

Rent/Mortgage:

Groceries:

Daycare:

Grooming:

Clothing:

Allowance:

Tuition:

Other:

NOTES

TRANSPORTATION EXPENSES

JUNE

Car Note:

Gas:

Maintenance:

Repairs:

Tolls:

Other:

NOTES

HEALTHCARE EXPENSES

JUNE

Health Insurance:

Life Insurance:

Dental Insurance:

Vision Insurance:

Copays:

Prescriptions:

Other:

NOTES

UTILITY EXPENSES

JUNE

Electricity:

Water:

Trash:

Sewage:

Internet:

Cable:

Phone:

Other:

NOTES

DEBTS

JUNE

Credit Card 1:

Credit Card 2:

Credit Card 3:

Personal Loan 1:

Personal Loan 2:

Student Loans:

NOTES

RECREATION EXPENSES

JUNE

Dining Out:

Social Events:

Entertainment:

Vacation Savings:

Other:

NOTES

MONTHLY BILL TRACKER

MONTH OF JUNE

TOTAL INCOME

OTHER INCOME / SAVINGS

BILL	DUE DATE	AMOUNT DUE	AMOUNT PAID	PAYMENT METHOD
TOTAL EXPENSES				

LIVING EXPENSES

JULY

Rent/Mortgage:

Groceries:

Daycare:

Grooming:

Clothing:

Allowance:

Tuition:

Other:

NOTES

TRANSPORTATION EXPENSES

JULY

Car Note:

Gas:

Maintenance:

Repairs:

Tolls:

Other:

NOTES

HEALTHCARE EXPENSES

JULY

Health Insurance:

Life Insurance:

Dental Insurance:

Vision Insurance:

Copays:

Prescriptions:

Other:

NOTES

UTILITY EXPENSES

JULY

Electricity:

Water:

Trash:

Sewage:

Internet:

Cable:

Phone:

Other:

NOTES

DEBTS

JULY

Credit Card 1:
Credit Card 2:
Credit Card 3:
Personal Loan 1:
Personal Loan 2:
Student Loans:

NOTES

RECREATION EXPENSES

JULY

Dining Out:
Social Events:
Entertainment:
Vacation Savings:
Other:

NOTES

MONTHLY BILL TRACKER

MONTH OF JULY				
TOTAL INCOME		**OTHER INCOME / SAVINGS**		

BILL	DUE DATE	AMOUNT DUE	AMOUNT PAID	PAYMENT METHOD
TOTAL EXPENSES				

LIVING EXPENSES

AUGUST

Rent/Mortgage:

Groceries:

Daycare:

Grooming:

Clothing:

Allowance:

Tuition:

Other:

NOTES

TRANSPORTATION EXPENSES

AUGUST

Car Note:

Gas:

Maintenance:

Repairs:

Tolls:

Other:

NOTES

HEALTHCARE EXPENSES

AUGUST

Health Insurance:

Life Insurance:

Dental Insurance:

Vision Insurance:

Copays:

Prescriptions:

Other:

NOTES

UTILITY EXPENSES

AUGUST

Electricity:

Water:

Trash:

Sewage:

Internet:

Cable:

Phone:

Other:

NOTES

DEBTS

AUGUST

Credit Card 1:

Credit Card 2:

Credit Card 3:

Personal Loan 1:

Personal Loan 2:

Student Loans:

NOTES

RECREATION EXPENSES

AUGUST

Dining Out:

Social Events:

Entertainment:

Vacation Savings:

Other:

NOTES

MONTHLY BILL TRACKER

MONTH OF AUGUST

TOTAL INCOME

OTHER INCOME / SAVINGS

BILL	DUE DATE	AMOUNT DUE	AMOUNT PAID	PAYMENT METHOD
TOTAL EXPENSES				

LIVING EXPENSES

SEPTEMBER

Rent/Mortgage:

Groceries:

Daycare:

Grooming:

Clothing:

Allowance:

Tuition:

Other:

NOTES

TRANSPORTATION EXPENSES

SEPTEMBER

Car Note:

Gas:

Maintenance:

Repairs:

Tolls:

Other:

NOTES

HEALTHCARE EXPENSES

SEPTEMBER

Health Insurance:

Life Insurance:

Dental Insurance:

Vision Insurance:

Copays:

Prescriptions:

Other:

NOTES

UTILITY EXPENSES

SEPTEMBER

Electricity:

Water:

Trash:

Sewage:

Internet:

Cable:

Phone:

Other:

NOTES

DEBTS

SEPTEMBER

Credit Card 1:

Credit Card 2:

Credit Card 3:

Personal Loan 1:

Personal Loan 2:

Student Loans:

NOTES

RECREATION EXPENSES

SEPTEMBER

Dining Out:

Social Events:

Entertainment:

Vacation Savings:

Other:

NOTES

MONTHLY BILL TRACKER

MONTH OF SEPTEMBER

TOTAL INCOME

OTHER INCOME / SAVINGS

BILL	DUE DATE	AMOUNT DUE	AMOUNT PAID	PAYMENT METHOD
TOTAL EXPENSES				

LIVING EXPENSES

OCTOBER

Rent/Mortgage:

Groceries:

Daycare:

Grooming:

Clothing:

Allowance:

Tuition:

Other:

NOTES

TRANSPORTATION EXPENSES

OCTOBER

Car Note:

Gas:

Maintenance:

Repairs:

Tolls:

Other:

NOTES

HEALTHCARE EXPENSES

OCTOBER

Health Insurance:

Life Insurance:

Dental Insurance:

Vision Insurance:

Copays:

Prescriptions:

Other:

NOTES

UTILITY EXPENSES

OCTOBER

Electricity:

Water:

Trash:

Sewage:

Internet:

Cable:

Phone:

Other:

NOTES

DEBTS

OCTOBER

Credit Card 1:

Credit Card 2:

Credit Card 3:

Personal Loan 1:

Personal Loan 2:

Student Loans:

NOTES

RECREATION EXPENSES

OCTOBER

Dining Out:

Social Events:

Entertainment:

Vacation Savings:

Other:

NOTES

MONTHLY BILL TRACKER

MONTH OF OCTOBER

TOTAL INCOME

OTHER INCOME / SAVINGS

BILL	DUE DATE	AMOUNT DUE	AMOUNT PAID	PAYMENT METHOD
TOTAL EXPENSES				

LIVING EXPENSES

NOVEMBER

Rent/Mortgage:

Groceries:

Daycare:

Grooming:

Clothing:

Allowance:

Tuition:

Other:

NOTES

TRANSPORTATION EXPENSES

NOVEMBER

Car Note:

Gas:

Maintenance:

Repairs:

Tolls:

Other:

NOTES

HEALTHCARE EXPENSES

NOVEMBER

Health Insurance:

Life Insurance:

Dental Insurance:

Vision Insurance:

Copays:

Prescriptions:

Other:

NOTES

UTILITY EXPENSES

NOVEMBER

Electricity:

Water:

Trash:

Sewage:

Internet:

Cable:

Phone:

Other:

NOTES

DEBTS

NOVEMBER

Credit Card 1:

Credit Card 2:

Credit Card 3:

Personal Loan 1:

Personal Loan 2:

Student Loans:

NOTES

RECREATION EXPENSES

NOVEMBER

Dining Out:

Social Events:

Entertainment:

Vacation Savings:

Other:

NOTES

MONTHLY BILL TRACKER

MONTH OF NOVEMBER

TOTAL INCOME			OTHER INCOME / SAVINGS	

BILL	DUE DATE	AMOUNT DUE	AMOUNT PAID	PAYMENT METHOD
TOTAL EXPENSES				

LIVING EXPENSES

DECEMBER

Rent/Mortgage:

Groceries:

Daycare:

Grooming:

Clothing:

Allowance:

Tuition:

Other:

NOTES

TRANSPORTATION EXPENSES

DECEMBER

Car Note:

Gas:

Maintenance:

Repairs:

Tolls:

Other:

NOTES

HEALTHCARE EXPENSES

DECEMBER

Health Insurance:

Life Insurance:

Dental Insurance:

Vision Insurance:

Copays:

Prescriptions:

Other:

NOTES

UTILITY EXPENSES

DECEMBER

Electricity:

Water:

Trash:

Sewage:

Internet:

Cable:

Phone:

Other:

NOTES

DEBTS

DECEMBER

Credit Card 1:

Credit Card 2:

Credit Card 3:

Personal Loan 1:

Personal Loan 2:

Student Loans:

NOTES

RECREATION EXPENSES

DECEMBER

Dining Out:

Social Events:

Entertainment:

Vacation Savings:

Other:

NOTES

MONTHLY BILL TRACKER

MONTH OF DECEMBER

TOTAL INCOME

OTHER INCOME / SAVINGS

BILL	DUE DATE	AMOUNT DUE	AMOUNT PAID	PAYMENT METHOD
TOTAL EXPENSES				